A maid bastes the roasting meat with one hand and with the other appears to be adjusting the chain from the jack. Saucepans sit on the hob and trivet of the range and a large oval-bellied pot hangs from a chimney crane over the fire. In the foreground a young man is being taught how to carve meat. (From William A. Henderson's 'The Housekeeper's Instructor', fifth edition, 1795.)

OLD COOKING UTENSILS

David J. Eveleigh

Shire Publications Ltd

CONTENTS

Published in 1994 by Shire Publications Ltd, Cromwell House, Church Street, Princes Risborough, Buckinghamshire HP27 9AA, UK.

Printed in Great Britain by CIT Printing Services, Press Buildings, Merlins Bridge, Haverfordwest, Dyfed SA61 1XF.

British Library Cataloguing in Publication Data: Eveleigh, David J. Old cooking utensils. — (Shire album; 177) 1. Kitchen utensils — Collectors and collecting. I. Title 683'.82 TX656. ISBN 0-85263-812-4.

ACKNOWLEDGEMENTS
Thanks are due to my former colleagues at the Museum of English Rural Life for their help; to Kate Gilmour for producing the copies from the trade catalogues; to Ron Mason, and to June Bamford for typing the manuscript. The line drawings are of objects from the collections at Blaise Castle House Museum, Bristol. Illustrations on the following pages are acknowledged to: Blaise Castle House Museum, City of Bristol Museum and Art Gallery, pages 3, 4 (lower), 5 (upper), 7, 8 (lower), 12, 13, 16 (upper right and lower), 17 (upper and lower), 18 (lower), 19 (upper), 22 (lower), 23, 25, 29, 31; the Brotherton Library, University of Leeds, page 1; the Museum of English Rural Life, pages 4 (upper), 5 (lower), 6, 8 (upper), 9, 10, 11, 14, 15, 17 (centre), 18 (upper), 19 (lower), 20, 24 (lower), 26, 28 (lower); the Science Museum, London, Crown copyright, page 21.

COVER: *A kitchen scene painted by William Locke (1767-1847).*

BELOW: *A wrought iron dutch crown, diameter 330 mm (13 inches).*

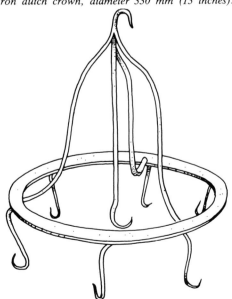

A late nineteenth-century stoneware bread bin with tinplate lid made by Doulton and Company, Lambeth, London.

STORING AND PRESERVING

Until refrigerators became generally available most fresh foods would not last above a few days and mainly needed to be protected from flies, insects and rodents. Fresh meat was stored in wooden cupboards or *safes* which were pierced with holes or made with other means of ventilation so that air could circulate and prevent the formation of mould. Nineteenth-century safes were commonly made with panels of wire gauze or perforated zinc. Meat safes were a familiar sight in kitchens and pantries.

Game hooks were a common fixture in the larders of larger houses. The hooks were often arranged on circular iron hoops called *dutch crowns*. Bread *flakes* or *creels,* large wooden frames hung from the ceiling, were once widely used for storing home-baked bread out of the reach of rats and mice. By the mid nineteenth century earthenware crocks or bins made of tinplate or enamelled iron were generally used for storing bread.

Eggs were sometimes kept in open baskets of wire or willow hung from the ceiling, but simple wooden racks were also used. Salt was stored in earthenware salt jars and in wooden salt boxes with lids attached by a strip of leather. For spices there were small chests of drawers, cylindrical wooden containers which unscrewed into several separate compartments and tinplate boxes with internal divisions for each spice. Until the eighteenth century domestic storage relied heavily on coopered vessels, but these gradually gave way to stoneware jars with knobbed lids and tinplate canisters which were particularly used for tea, flour and sugar.

Most foods to be stored for long periods needed to be preserved. The meat of animals slaughtered in the autumn because of the shortage of winter feed was salted. The pig was the preferred salting animal and long after the problem of winter feed had been solved the widespread practice amongst ordinary people of keeping a pig ensured that curing remained an essential domestic skill well into the nineteenth century. Methods of salting varied from one region to another, but all required a wooden tub or trough in which the meat was salted. These appear in many inven-

3

ABOVE LEFT: *An egg basket of wire, believed to be earlier than 1850: it can hold almost two dozen eggs.*

ABOVE RIGHT: *A salt box made of pine. These were usually hung near the fireplace to keep the salt dry.*

BELOW: *Spice boxes. (Left) Two wooden containers which unscrew into separate compartments, mid nineteenth century. (Right) A tinplate container with space for six different spices, with a nutmeg grater in the centre.*

(From left to right) A salt jar, earthenware with dark brown lead glaze and white slip trailed decoration including the word 'salt' on the back. Stoneware jar with knobbed lid by Price of Bristol. Two stoneware storage jars with lustrous dark brown glaze; the larger one was used to store flour.

tories along with carcase hangers and cleavers. Charles Cleark, a small farmer of Writtle, Essex, left 'one Salting trough for Bacon, 4s' in 1659. The troughs were large enough to accommodate an entire side or flitch of bacon and had grooves cut in the base for the brine to drain away. Salting took several weeks while salt was regularly rubbed into the flesh to absorb the moisture. Curing was sometimes completed by hanging the meat in the chimney over a wood fire. As the nineteenth century advanced domestic salting declined, but as late as the 1880s pigs were still slaughtered and cured by the cottagers of Juniper Hill, the tiny hamlet in north Oxfordshire which was the setting of Flora Thompson's *Lark Rise to Candleford*.

Apart from apples, which needed only to be laid apart in a cool, dry place, most other fruits required thorough preparation if they were to keep, usually by bottling with sugar or jam making. The bottling jars were tightly sealed with corks covered in melted resin or wax.

A wooden ham trough lined with lead. From Drayton, near Abingdon, and last used during the Second World War.

ABOVE: *A sheet copper preserving pan.*

Jam or marmalade was boiled in wide pans of copper or brass which were expensive and often among the most cherished kitchen utensils. After about 1850 cheaper enamelled iron pans were introduced but were disparaged because the sugar or syrup was liable to boil over too quickly. By this time, however, the preserving pan had lost some of its importance, especially among poorer housewives who turned to the cheap, ready-made jams and marmalades available from the increasing number of corner shops.

LEFT: *A green glass jam jar, early twentieth century, used at Turville Heath, Buckinghamshire, for storing home-made jam which was sealed with paper fastened with string.*

A wrought iron chopper flanked by late nineteenth-century Sheffield-made choppers of cast steel.

FOOD PREPARATION

Considerable time and energy used to be taken up preparing the basic ingredients for meals and a wide range of simple hand implements for grinding, chopping and shredding were once indispensable to the cook. Chopping knives were used for heavier work. Most choppers had a rectangular wrought iron blade linked to a horizontal wooden handle by iron supports at one or both ends. In the second half of the nineteenth century they were manufactured in large numbers by the Sheffield edge-tool makers in cast steel with a single central support to a handle which was usually attractively turned from beech or mahogany. Such choppers were used on wooden chopping boards, although some knives with curved blades were intended for use inside wooden bowls or mortars.

The mortar and pestle were used to pulverise sugar, spices and many other foods. Mortars are among the most frequently listed items of kitchen equipment in inventories of the sixteenth, seventeenth and eighteenth centuries. The majority of those recorded were made of brass or bronze, but pestles and mortars or iron, wood and marble also feature in inventories prior to about 1750. Many surviving brass examples are relatively small but Thomas Jones, a gentleman from Wellington, Shropshire, owned a brass mortar weighing 28 pounds (12.7 kg) in 1692. With brass then worth 7d per pound this mortar was valued at sixteen shillings and fourpence. Iron and wooden mortars and pestles were much cheaper. Mortars made of earthenware, produced by Wedgwood, were another cheap alternative available in the nineteenth century. Mrs Beeton's *Shilling Cookery Book* of the 1880s recommends a Wedgwood mortar and pestle costing three shillings and ninepence for the smallest (the author might well have said poorest) homes, as against an expenditure of fifteen shillings for a marble mortar 'suitable for any mansion'.

There were many other utensils designed to prepare particular foods. Graters were in use by the seventeenth century to provide bread crumbs which had many uses in cooking. They were generally made of tinplated iron. Earlier examples were hand punched but by the nineteenth century machine punching provided uniform perforations and it was common for graters to be provided with several different grating textures. Small pocket-sized graters were used for nutmeg. Lemon squeezers frequently took the form of two pieces of wood, jointed at one end, between which a half lemon could be squeezed. Another type consisted of an inverted fluted cone sur-

7

ABOVE: *A mortar and pestle made by Wedgwood, formerly used for making mint sauce.*

BELOW: *Tinplate graters. (Left) A pocket-size nutmeg grater. (Right) Two machine-stamped graters with several different grating textures.*

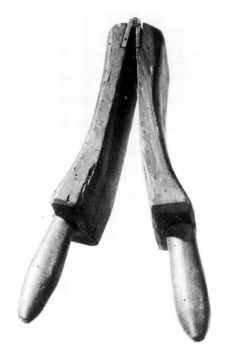

rounded by a reservoir to collect the juice; these were found in tinplate and earthenware, and, from the late nineteenth century, pressed glass. Other specialised implements included apple corers, cucumber slicers, steak beaters and potato mashers, following the adoption of potatoes as a staple of the British diet in the eighteenth century. There were also many general accessories, such as whisks, sieves, colanders and funnels.

With the exception of pestles and mortars, small utensils were rarely of any value and seldom appear in documentary sources before 1800. However, in the nineteenth century references to the smaller items increase markedly. To some extent this may be attributed to the growing popularity of French dishes amongst the middle and upper classes and a greater emphasis on the flavouring and appearance of food. Extensive advertising in newspapers, periodicals and the advice contained in such influential books of household management as those compiled by Thomas Webster and Isabella

Beeton turned the furnishing of kitchens, from the range down to the cucumber slice, into a serious business for the middle classes. It was on this affluent and receptive market that mechanical accessories made such an obvious impact from the 1850s.

Some mechanical implements were in use as early as the seventeenth century. Steel mills for grinding malt for making beer were common in the seventeenth century and only disappeared when beer was displaced by tea as the national drink in the eighteenth century. The introduction of another new beverage, coffee, led to the appearance of coffee mills from about 1700. Samuel Codrington, a gentleman from Frampton Cotterell near Bristol, left one amongst the contents of his study when he died in 1709. Coffee was then a luxury drink, confined to the wealthy, and even the apparatus connected with the drink was accorded some status. Eighteenth-century coffee mills are usually beautifully turned wooden vessels, typically lignum vitae or maho-

A steak beater made of beech.

A potato masher.

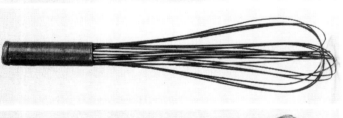

A wire whisk. Early whisks were made from bunches of twigs.

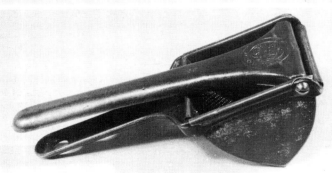

A cast-iron potato masher or ricer, first patented in 1880 by A. Kendrick and Sons, West Bromwich.

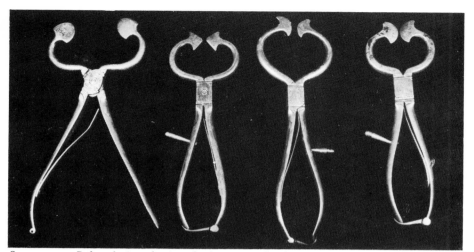

Sugar cutters. Before the introduction of cube sugar, refined sugar was made in the form of a large cone called a sugar loaf, which was broken into smaller pieces by sugar cutters made of iron or steel.

gany, incorporating a conical cutter which was turned by a detachable crank handle. When not in use the handle was folded up, stored inside the mill and an attractive wooden lid screwed in place. Household inventories show that the mills were normally kept in the parlour (or the study) but rarely the kitchen. In 1815 Archibald Kenrick took out a patent for cheaper coffee mills made in cast iron and these were made in large numbers by Kenricks and other firms throughout the nineteenth century.

There was little progress in the development of other mechanical kitchen implements until after the Great Exhibition in 1851, which opened an era of numerous international trade fairs ideal for their promotion. After one exhibition in 1854 the *Times* praised the 'ingenious

A brass colander, formerly used in Reading. Colanders were also made in tinplate, enamel and earthenware.

11

Coffee mills. (From left to right) An eighteenth-century type made of lignum vitae with the crank handle in place and the domed lid removed; cast iron mill by W. B. Bullock and Company; cast iron mill by A. Kenrick and Sons.

mincing machine' exhibited by Nye and Company of Soho, London. Another observer remarked that it could mince 8 pounds (3.6 kg) of meat in four minutes and added, 'this is a little item every husband ought to carry home to his wife'. This was advice for the well off as the smallest model cost a guinea, more than a week's wages for the labouring majority.

By 1860 sausage making machines were being made by Nye and by A. Lyons, another London firm. Several devices such as apple corers and peelers and Monroe's egg beater originated in the United States. Other labour saving devices which followed were mechanical choppers (which resembled beam engines), bean slicers, orange slicers for marmalade making, raisin stoners, potato mashers and rotary graters. Most of these were made of cast iron until the late nineteenth century when cast aluminium appeared as a lighter alternative.

A marmalade cutter and vegetable slicer from the furnishing ironmongery catalogue of Gardiner Sons and Company of Bristol, about 1910.

No. H 8049.
MARMALADE CUTTER.
16/- ea.

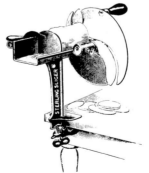

No. H 8047.
VEGETABLE SLICER.
8/6 ea.

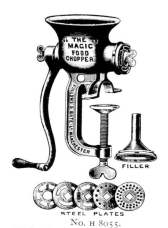

No. H 8055.
With 5 Perforated Plates as shown
Nos.   o   I   Ia   2a
       4/- 5/- 7/6 12/-
Sausage Fillers 1/- 1/- 1/6 1/6 extra

No. H 8056.—MINCING MACHINE
Size   o   I   Ia   2   3
       5/6 6/6 7/9 9/6 14/- ea

No. H 8057.
Coated with pure tin.
With 3 Perforated Plates and Cramp,
5/6 each

No. H 8058.
MEAT AND SUET CHOPPER.
Size   I   Ia   2   3   3a
       14/- 16/9 19/6 28/- 40/- ea.

No. H 8059.—MEAT AND SUET CHOPPER
8-in. cylinder, 25/- ea. ; 10-in. 35/9 ea.

No. H 8060.—POTATO CHIPPER
Small size. 4/3 ea. ; Large size, 6/6 ea

The range of mechanical mincing machines and meat choppers from the Gardiner catalogue.

LEFT: *A press for compressing cooked meat.*

BELOW: *Kitchen scales were one of the most important items of cooking equipment. The earliest type consisted of two pans suspended from a pivoted beam but from the early nineteenth century these beamscales gave way to cast-iron weighing machines like this one illustrated in J. C. Loudon's 'Cottage, Farm and Villa Architecture', 1833. Although not as accurate as beamscales, they were quick to use. Spring balance scales with attractive dials of brass made by Salters and other scale makers became popular in the late nineteenth century. Weights were of various types: bar weights in cast iron, circular flat weights made of either cast brass or cast iron, or bell weights, the most expensive type, which were usually made only in cast brass.*

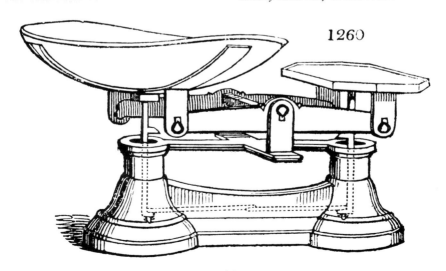

1260

Cauldrons. (Left) A seventeenth-century bronze cauldron. (Right) A cast iron cauldron, of the eighteenth or nineteenth century.

BOILING, STEWING AND FRYING

Boiling was the simplest and most widely practised method of cooking. Large boiling vessels, described variously as crocks, cauldrons, kettles, boilers and furnaces constitute the most widely found cooking utensils prior to 1800. They were used at every social level but amongst the poor especially were regularly employed to prepare an entire meal. Meat was placed in a pot of boiling water, followed later by vegetables and a pudding which were wrapped in cloths and nets. This method of cooking was still used by many cottagers in the late nineteenth century, and is vividly described by Flora Thompson in *Lark Rise to Candleford*.

Despite the variety of names, there were basically just two main types of boiling vessel; the *cauldron* and the *kettle*. Both had a long ancestry. Metal cauldrons were first used in Britain about 1000 BC during the late bronze age, and kettles originated in the Anglo-Saxon *cytel*. Cauldrons were round bellied and round bottomed, and by the middle ages were being made with three legs which gave them stability and enabled them to stand in the fire. They were also provided with two ears close to the rim by which they could be suspended over the hearth. Cauldrons were always made of cast metal, unlike kettles which were made from sheet metal, usually brass, hammered by hand to form a straighter sided, open-top vessel. From the early eighteenth century, large numbers of brass kettles were manufactured using water powered hammers. In the nineteenth century kettles made of copper or tinplate rather than brass, and of an oblong or oval shape with close fitting lids, were used for boiling ham or fish. By the nineteenth century, the kettle, in an altered shape, was chiefly associated with the boiling of water for tea. The first tea kettles with spouts date from the 1690s, but as tea was then a luxury drink, the first examples were made in silver. An early instance of a tea kettle lower in the social strata occurs in the 1723 inventory of Abraham Boosey of Writtle, Essex. It was only later in the century that tea kettles were established as a familiar part of the kitchen.

Most cauldrons recorded in sixteenth and seventeenth century inventories were cast in a metal commonly described by contemporaries as 'crock brass' or 'bell metal'. This was an alloy of copper and tin, similar to bronze, although usually containing quantities of lead and zinc. There are a few inventories which list

15

LEFT: *A brass hanging kettle, based on the drawing in Randle Holmes's 'Academy of Armoury', 1688.*

RIGHT: *A tinplate ham kettle of the early twentieth century, formerly used in Bristol for cooking ham, which was soaked overnight in the kettle, drained and then boiled for twenty minutes per pound (0.45 kg). The kettle contains a close-fitting perforated tray on which the ham was lifted from the water.*

cauldrons made of iron, but these were rare. Although cast iron was cheap it was of poor quality until Abraham Darby developed smelting with coke in place of charcoal after 1709 and began large scale production of cooking pots, kettles and frying pans. Of his cast iron bellied pots Darby proclaimed, 'in regard to their cheapness [they] may be of great advantage to the poor of this our kingdom'. As other foundries adopted coke smelting and introduced further refinements, cast iron cauldrons gradually replaced those made of bell metal.

Tea kettles. (From left) A copper kettle, probably early nineteenth century; a square hob kettle, mid or late nineteenth century; a cast iron kettle with tinplate lid.

By the close of the eighteenth century production was centred in the towns of the West Midlands and manufacturers there introduced new types of vessels. In 1779, John Izon, a Birmingham ironfounder who later moved to West Bromwich, purchased John Taylor's patent of the same year for making oval bellied cast iron pots which were finished with a neat rim around the top and tinned on the inside. Cleaner and lighter than the old cauldrons, they were still cheap. As their introduction coincided with the addition of iron hobs and hot plates to kitchen ranges the ironfounders dispensed with the three legs of the traditional pot and gave them flat bases so they could sit comfortably on the hob. They were also made with a bail handle for hanging in the open-hearth chimney. These new oval pots were an immediate success and, during the nineteenth century the three legged cauldron disappeared from use. In 1844 Thomas Webster could write that the cauldron was still 'generally used in the north of Scotland for making broth, but in London used chiefly for boiling pitch'.

ABOVE RIGHT: *A cast iron, oval bellied boiling pot, of 6 gallons (27.3 litres) capacity with tinplate lid, by A. Kenrick and Sons.*

RIGHT: *A cast iron digester, of 3 gallons (13.6 litres) capacity, by A. Kenrick and Sons.*

BELOW: *(From left to right) A bell-metal skillet by Roger Rice of Bristol, active from 1740 to about 1754; a copper stewpan from the Mansion House, Bristol, the residence of the lord mayor; a bell-metal saucepan.*

Cast iron saucepans. (Left) A 7 pint (4 litre) pan by E. Pugh and Company, Wednesbury. (Right) A 7 quart (8 litre) pan by A. Kenrick and Sons, used until the mid 1950s.

Throughout the nineteenth century the manufacture of oval bellied boiling pots in cast iron was dominated by several West Midland foundries. Particularly prominent were Thomas and Charles Clark of Wolverhampton, founded in 1795; from 1805, Archibald Kenrick of Spon Lane, West Bromwich and Joseph and Jesse Siddons, also in West Bromwich, who started business in 1846. The names of these makers can often be seen cast on the base of boiling pots and many other cooking vessels: tea kettles, for example, and large tea boilers capable

In cold weather home-brewed beer was often warmed in the fire using ale mullers. (From the left) A conical type which was pushed into the top of the fire, copper with a mahogany handle; a tinplate slipper-type muller which was pushed into the embers on the hearth; a copper slipper-type.

18

of holding several gallons and fitted with brass taps and stock pots used to prepare stock for soups and gravies. By the 1830s Kenricks were also producing an early form of pressure cooker known as a *digester*. The idea was not new and had been demonstrated before the Royal Society in 1681 by Denis Papin, a French physician. But the method was not exploited until Kenricks, by producing it in cheap cast iron, assured its success. The digester was a sturdy cast iron pot with a domed lid fitted with a simple weighted safety valve. The valve provided the only means of escape for surplus steam as the lid was held in place by three lugs. Pressure built up inside the pot raising the temperature at which the water boiled and at the same time forcing superheated steam through the food. Cooking time was reduced and so was the amount of fuel required — another important consideration for the poor. In the 1880s a 2 gallon (9 litre) digester could be bought for 5s 6d — less than a third of the price of a copper tea kettle.

For boiling smaller quantities skillets had been used for many centuries and remained common until the eighteenth century. They had three short legs and a long straight handle so they could be placed directly on the fire. Some were made of earthenware, although few survive complete, others of sheet brass or of bell metal, an alloy of copper and tin. Bell metal skillets were made in large numbers. Late seventeenth-century examples often bear inscriptions such as 'Pittie the Pore' and 'Ye wages of sin is death' : these may reflect the radical religious and political beliefs of their makers rather than mere sentiment. Eighteenth-century skillet handles often bear the name of the maker: for example 'Warner', a London brass founder, and 'Wasborough', a firm involved in brass founding in Bristol from about 1753 until 1847.

In the eighteenth century, skillets gave way to flat-bottomed saucepans which were placed on circular trivets or the hobs of the range. In *The Art of Cookery Made Plain and Easy*, a well-known eighteenth-century cookery book written by Hannah Glasse and first published in 1747, the author lists only two recipes

ABOVE: *A wrought iron chafing dish. Chafing dishes held burning charcoal or coal and were used for the gentle heating of food and drink.*

BELOW: *A nineteenth-century oval frying pan, copper with an iron handle. From a cottage at Ickford, Buckinghamshire.*

19

LEFT: *A cast iron hanging frying pan with a pouring lip.*

RIGHT: *A fish slice, copper with an iron handle. From Papplewick Hall, Nottinghamshire, believed to date from the 1860s.*

which required a skillet.

Mostly she recommends the use of saucepans. These were available in cast brass with rolled iron handles or in sheet copper, a metal which was increasingly used for kitchen utensils during the eighteenth century. Valued for providing an instantaneous and even transmission of heat, copper was expensive and it was usually only found in wealthier households. To guard against the poisonous compounds of copper which some foods could create, copper vessels were always tinned on the inside.

There was one exception, however: preserving pans could not be tinned as the boiling point of sugar is too close to the melting point of tin. The use of cheaper tinplate pans, made of sheet iron coated with tin, also expanded after 1700 but these were vulnerable to the intense heat of the large kitchen ranges which could melt the tin coating, exposing the iron, which would soon rust. More durable were cast-iron saucepans, which were widely used in Victorian kitchens and after about 1840 were also available with enamelled surfaces. Steamers with perforated bases, placed on top of saucepans, had appeared before 1800.

Stewing required a gentle even heat and for this a separate brick stove burning charcoal was often used in preference to the main kitchen grate until the development in the nineteenth century of kitchen ranges enclosed on top with a hot plate. Stewpans, which came with lids, were generally shallower than saucepans and preferably made of copper. In large households stewpans were often placed in a *bain-marie*, a long pan filled with hot water, which allowed the contents of the stewpans to be kept hot without any risk of burning or loss of flavour.

Frying was a simple and economical method of cooking particularly suited to the poor as it required little fuel and only a cheap iron frying pan. It was also useful when the fire was too low for boiling or roasting. Most frying pans were made of wrought iron, although they were also found in cast iron and copper. For use over an open fire frying pans were often fitted with handles 40 inches (1 metre) long so that they could be held at a distance from the heat. Others were made with a semicircular handle so they could be suspended over an open fire. Other types included oval-shaped frying pans for fish, smaller sizes for omelette making and shallow straight-sided versions used to sauté fillets of meat.

The kitchen from 'Modern Domestic Cookery', 1855, based on the work of Mrs Rundell. The engraving shows the typical arrangement of a large kitchen of the time. The range has a smoke jack for turning the spits, although a small joint is suspended from a bottle jack.

ROASTING, BROILING AND TOASTING

Before about 1800, the generous dimensions of the average kitchen fireplace produced a large surface area of radiant heat ideal for broiling, toasting and especially for roasting. In 1748, Peter Kalm, a Swedish visitor to England wrote, 'Roast beef is the Englishman's delice and principal dish ... Englishmen understand almost better than any other people the art of roasting a joint'. Inventories corroborate Kalm's observation: most list roasting equipment and only the poor did not eat roast meat regularly.

The distinctive flavour of meat roasted before a fire was achieved by quickly sealing the outer surface in order to retain the natural juices. The meat was rotated on a long horizontal iron spit in front of the fire, presenting each surface in turn to the greatest heat. The meat was usually secured to the spit by a two pronged fork, although it was sometimes contained within a basket spit. Smaller spits were used for birds such as larks. The spit was supported by a pair of large firedogs with hooks called *andirons*, or alternatively by *cobirons*, long bars with

hooks which were leaned against the back of the fireplace. Both ceased to be used after the introduction of coal burning ranges which had hooks for the spit attached to the two front uprights of the grate. The fat which dripped from the joint was collected in a *dripping pan* and poured back over using a *basting ladle*. As ash and cinders tended to fall into the dripping pan it was not uncommon to find both pans and ladles fitted with strainers to separate the ash from the fat. *Roasting screens*, also known as *hasteners* or *dutch ovens*, appeared in the early eighteenth century. They were made of tinplate and stood in front of the fire, the bright surface reflecting the heat, reducing cooking time and saving fuel. They were made in various sizes, the larger ones standing on three legs. Most incorporated a dripping pan and a door in the back for basting. Large *fleshforks* were essential for handling the meat.

In the middle ages *turnspits* were employed to turn the spit by hand. The spits were cranked at one end to make the turning easier but it was hot and arduous

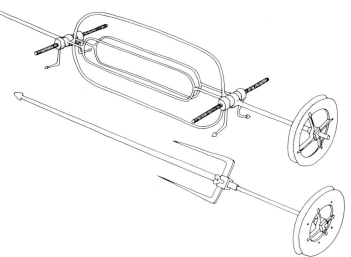

A steel cradle spit (top) and a steel spit with sliding fork (bottom). From Henbury Manor, Bristol.

work and a few seconds inattention by the turnspit could result in burnt meat. Turnspit dogs, which were made to run endlessly inside a wooden wheel fitted beside the fireplace, are recorded before 1600. An endless chain ran from the axle or spindle of the revolving wheel to a grooved wheel on the spit. *Dog wheels* were used throughout the seventeenth and eighteenth centuries, but were never as common as weight-driven *spit-jacks* which were introduced about 1600. Weight-jacks had a weight on a line which was wound up around a barrel. As it descended, the barrel rotated. A chain transferred the motion to the spit and to ensure it turned evenly the barrel was geared to a flywheel. The gear arrange-

Weight-driven spit-jacks. (From the left) A wrought iron spit-jack, possibly late seventeenth century, with the flywheel missing; a wrought iron jack, eighteenth or early nineteenth century; a brassed faced jack inscribed 'Eva Tregony'. This may be the Richard Eva who was recorded as a clockmaker in Falmouth, Cornwall, in 1775.

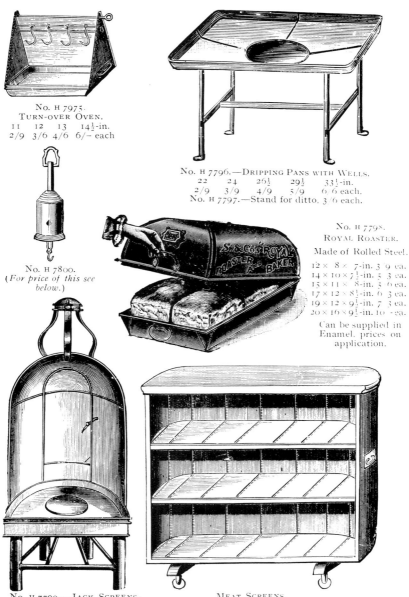

No. H 7975.
TURN-OVER OVEN.
11   12   13   14½-in.
2/9 3/6 4/6 6/- each

No. H 7796.—DRIPPING PANS WITH WELLS.
22   24   26½   29½   33½-in.
2/9   3/9   4/9   5/9   6/6 each.
No. H 7797.—Stand for ditto. 3/6 each.

No. H 7800.
(*For price of this see below.*)

No. H 7798.
ROYAL ROASTER.

Made of Rolled Steel.

12 × 8 × 7-in. 3/9 ea.
14 × 10 × 7½-in. 5/3 ea.
15 × 11 × 8-in. 5/6 ea.
17 × 12 × 8½-in. 6/3 ea.
19 × 12 × 9½-in. 7/3 ea.
20 × 16 × 9½-in. 10/- ea.

Can be supplied in Enamel, prices on application.

No. H 7799.—JACK SCREENS.
Small 15/9 ; Med. 20/- ; Lrg. 28/-
No. H 7800.—Brass Jack for do.

MEAT SCREENS.
No. H 7790.—Wood, Tin Lined,
3-ft. 6-in., 57/- 4-ft., 80/- 4-ft. 6-in., 102/- ea.

Reflecting screens, a dripping pan and other roasting equipment, from the catalogue of Gardiner Sons and Company of Bristol, about 1910.

23

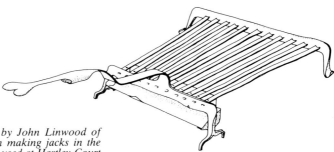

ment was simple enough to be copied by local smiths and after about 1660 the use of jacks spread rapidly.

From the early eighteenth century weight-jacks were replaced in larger kitchens by *smoke-jacks.* These had a metal fan set in the throat of the chimney which was turned by the strong upward draught from the fire; a train of gears, pulleys and chains transferred the motion to the spit. Smoke-jacks did not require winding up like weight-jacks and a further advantage was that several spits could be operated simultaneously enabling the cook to present several roast dishes on the menu. In complete contrast, spring operated jacks, designed to rotate smaller joints on a vertical axis without the aid of a spit, appeared in the second half of the eighteenth century. Joseph Merlin patented one in 1773 and adapted it to the roasting screen. By 1790, vertical spring roasting jacks, which from their shape were popularly known as *bottle-jacks,* had appeared. The reduced width of the grates in most nineteenth-century ranges encouraged the spread of vertical roasting and bottle-jacks enjoyed tremendous popularity. Although in the 1880s a bottle-jack could be bought for as little as 6s 6d the poor usually made do with a piece of twisted string.

Open fire roasting required a lot of fuel and it was not uncommon for the less well off to send their joint to the baker to be oven roasted although meat cooked in a baking oven, deprived of radiant heat and circulating air came out sodden and smelling of burnt fat. It was not until after 1795, when Count Rumford, an American inventor, introduced a specially adapted ventilation system, that roast-

Toasters: a hand-held steel toasting fork (left), a standing toaster with sliding frame of spikes (right) and a firebar toaster with an adjustable two-pronged fork (front).

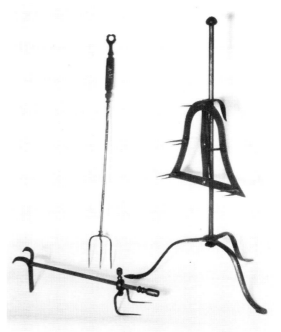

ing ovens were fitted to ranges. As closed ranges developed during the nineteenth century more roasting ovens were fitted as open fire roasting became impossible for all but the smallest pieces of meat. By about 1900 open fire roasting was in decline and within a few decades had virtually disappeared due to the general adoption of gas and electric cookers.

Smaller cuts of meat were *broiled* on a *gridiron,* an open iron grid which stood on four feet over a clear bright fire, free of smoke. As in roasting, the surface was quickly hardened forming a crust which retained the juices. Gridirons were usually cheaply made in wrought iron and were among the most common cooking utensils until the demise of open kitchen fires. With the increasing use of kitchen grates in the eighteenth century, gridirons were made with splayed rear legs so they could rest on the top firebar. It was important that the gridiron was kept slanting towards the cook so that as little fat as possible fell into the fire. Later examples were made with grooved bars which channelled the fat into a reservoir by

the handle. After about 1850 enamelled gridirons and some with the extra refinement of a revolving grid were made by T. and C. Clark and other ironfounders. *Steak tongs,* which did not pierce the meat, were sometimes used to handle the meat in broiling.

Small cuts of meat, kippers, cheese, bread and muffins were toasted. The simplest *toasters* were hand held two pronged forks, but a wide variety of types were made to stand in front of the fire. Small standing toasters were made with a fork and a drip tray for meat and with two vertical loops, like a toast rack, for bread. Taller versions suitable for ranges developed. Many took the form of a frame of spikes which could be adjusted up and down a tripod mounted stem. Alternatively, there were toasters which hooked on to the top firebar of the grate; these usually had a fork fitted to a slide so that the distance from the fire could be adjusted. In Scotland, decorative wrought iron toasters were used to toast flat scones or bannocks, an unleavened bread.

25

Oatcake making from Walker's 'Costume of Yorkshire', 1814. The batter has been mixed in an earthenware pancheon, and the housewife is spreading the mix on a riddle board. A built-in bakestone is used and the finished oatcakes are hung from the ceiling on a creel.

BAKING

Originally ovens were associated exclusively with baking. From the sixteenth and seventeenth centuries most substantial homes in the countryside were built with a wall oven which generally consisted of a circular domed cavity reached by a small rectangular opening; from their shape they are sometimes described as 'beehive ovens'. Faggots were burned inside the oven to heat the masonry or brick lining, then the embers were carefully spread around the floor to ensure it was heated evenly before being raked out. The problems of gauging the temperature and periodic reheating during a long baking were not resolved until the introduction of iron ovens with a grate directly beneath, from about 1750. 'Perpetual ovens' as they were appropriately known could be kept hot indefinitely, and as a flue ran from the grate around the sides of the oven a more even heat was assured. From the 1770s iron ovens (although not always with a surrounding flue) were attached to the main kitchen grate forming the typical nineteenth century kitchen range.

In the West Country, and to a lesser extent in South Wales, the brick or masonry oven was replaced by portable versions made of earthenware or 'cloam'. Production of these was centred in the north Devon pottery towns of Bideford, Barnstaple and Fremington, although they were also made at Calstock and Truro in Cornwall. They are recorded as early as about 1600 and continued in use until the early twentieth century. The last Truro ovens were made in 1937.

Cloam ovens were found in poorer homes but in other parts of Britain the less well off generally relied on methods of hearth baking. In Cornwall, northern England, Wales, Ireland and Scotland the three-legged cauldron was inverted over the item to be baked and hot embers piled up around the outside. From the late eighteenth century, the iron foundries produced shallow cast iron baking pots with lids. These were sometimes

26

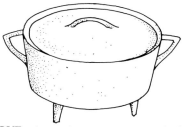

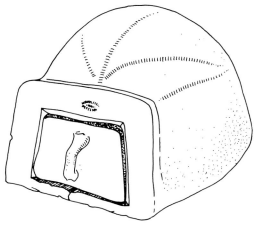

ABOVE: *A cast iron camp oven with three legs.*
RIGHT: *A cloam oven made by the Branham Pottery, Barnstaple, and removed from an early nineteenth-century house in Montpelier, Bristol.*
BELOW: *(Left) A wrought iron oven peel from Giles Green, near Hawkhurst, Kent, length 1490 mm (58 inches). (Right) A wrought iron ember rake with ash handle from Gloucestershire, length 1524 mm (60 inches).*

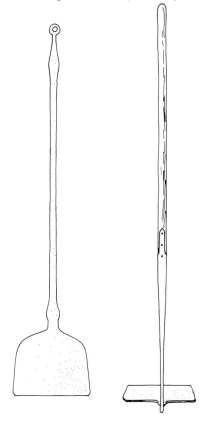

known as *camp ovens*, and in Yorkshire as *yetlings*.

Many farmhouse and cottage inventories from the sixteenth to the eighteenth centuries list the essential equipment of bread making: wooden tubs or troughs to knead the dough, moulding boards on which the loaves were shaped and bolting tubs used to sift the flour from the bran. The loaves were taken in and out of the oven on flat shovel-like implements of either wood or iron called *peels*. From the late eighteenth century these items were found less frequently in kitchens as domestic bread making declined. The first national food inquiry conducted by Dr Edward Smith in 1863 revealed that whilst bread was the chief article of subsistence amongst rural labourers only 20 per cent still baked their own.

By the mid nineteenth century domestic bread baking survived most strongly in the north where living conditions were generally better and cheap fuel in the form of coal was widely available. In common with the rest of upland north and west Britain there was also a flourishing tradition of unleavened bread made from barley, rye and oats which were better suited than wheat to the harsher climate. In Northumberland and Scotland unleavened bannocks were baked over the hearth on open wrought iron supports, usually circular in shape and termed *branders*. The bannocks were removed from the brander by *spurtles,* spatula-like implements made of wrought iron often in the form of a heart. In Wales and the Pennines, flat oatcakes were baked on a bakestone, a heated stone slab placed on the hearth, or, in larger houses, permanently fixed on brick or masonry supports with a fireplace underneath. Iron bakestones are recorded in some Yorkshire inventories of the mid seventeenth century and by the nineteenth had largely superseded those of stone. Iron bakestones, also known as *griddles* or *girdles,* consisted of thick circular plates of iron, usually about 12 inches (30 mm) diameter, which rested on the top bar or hob of a range or were suspended over the fire by a semicircular handle. Wooden slices were used to lift the oatcakes from the griddle.

Wooden mixing bowls, turned from elm or sycamore, were common as were *pancheons,* conical sided bowls of coarse country earthenware. From the mid nineteenth century, cream earthenware and stoneware mixing bowls were produced in ever increasing numbers and largely supplanted wooden vessels. Rolling pins for pastry were either convex or straight-sided and usually made of beech or sycamore. Glass rolling pins were also found and ridged wooden rollers were used in oatcake making areas to break the cake up for broths.

Pastry was cut to shape using *jiggers,* small cutting tools made of wood or brass with a revolving serrated wheel at one end and often a pastry crimper at the other, and circular tinplate cutters. More elaborate shapes, such as hearts or flowers, were used to make pastry decorations for pies or open tarts and to cut out biscuits. Pies were baked in oval dishes of earthenware or tinplate. These had wide rims so that pastry lids could be firmly attached to the edge. Raised pie moulds were used to shape the sides of straight sided pies. A common type consisted of a solid wooden cylinder, usually sycamore, around which the pastry was wrapped; when the mould was removed the space left was taken by the pie mixture. An alternative type which Mrs Beeton recommended for a raised pie of poultry or

game in 1861 was made of tinplate with removable sides and bottom. Plain square or round tinplate moulds were used to bake cakes and small round moulds called *patty pans* provided the support for mince pies and small tarts. Simple circular bands of tinplate were used to support the liquid batter of crumpets on the griddle.

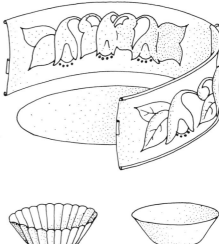

ABOVE: *A raised pie mould with an embossed design and two patty pans, plain and fluted, redrawn from Isabella Beeton's 'Book of Household Management', 1861.*

BELOW: *A cast iron griddle with a handle for suspension, used in Sunningdale, Berkshire.*

ABOVE: *Two seventeenth-century gingerbread moulds (left and right), an oak riddle board for oatcake making (centre rear), an elm mixing bowl (centre), and a convex rolling pin of beech (front).*

BELOW: *Tinplate pastry cutters and, below, two wooden pastry jiggers (left) and two smaller ones of cast brass (right).*

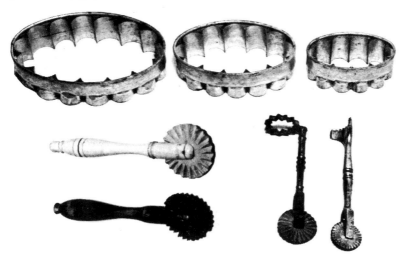

Elaborately carved wooden moulds bearing a fascinating range of subjects were found in many seventeenth and eighteenth century kitchens to shape gingerbread. In wealthier homes wafers, made from eggs, flour, milk, butter and yeast, were baked in *waffle irons,* which consisted of iron tongs with decoratively inscribed faces. They were heated in the fire, the batter applied to one of the two surfaces and then tightly clamped together to produce a paper-thin wafer. *Salamanders,* thick plates or discs of iron on the end of a long handle, were heated in the fire until they were red hot and then held over pastry and meringues to brown the surface without warming the inside.

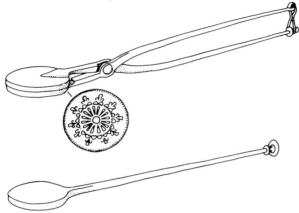

A wrought iron waffle iron (above) and a salamander (below).

COLD SWEETS

Decoratively presented cold sweets were popular among the well-off in the eighteenth and nineteenth centuries. Ice cream was made from fresh cream, eggs, sugar and fruit juice stirred together in a freezing pot submerged in a tub of ice. By the late nineteenth century small hand cranked ice cream makers were on the market. Most were priced between £1 and £3 but the 'Imperial Ice Cream Maker', advertised in the 1907 Army and Navy Stores catalogue, cost only 4s 11d. Ice cream was shaped in heavy pewter moulds which were made in a wide range of shapes.

Jellies were popular. Gelatine was obtained by boiling animal bones, sheeps' heads and, most commonly, calves' feet. Egg whites were added to clarify the liquid which was then strained through a linen or flannel jelly bag to separate the scum. Jelly bags were commonly suspended from the backs of two chairs, but in larger establishments specially made jelly frames were used. A 'jelly frame' is listed among the contents of the kitchen at Appledurcombe Park, the seat of Sir Richard Wasley, about 1780. The jelly bag was also used to strain the juice from the pulp of fresh fruit.

The earliest jelly moulds were made in Staffordshire white salt glaze in the 1730s. Later in the eighteenth century fine white earthenware or *creamware* moulds were produced by Wedgwood and some of these came in two parts: an outer mould and an inner core of cone, pyramid or wedge shape, which was delicately painted and left in the jelly when it was served. In the nineteenth century earthenware moulds in many shapes and bearing a vast range of subjects were made by potteries in Staffordshire and Derbyshire. Some of the most elaborate moulds were made of copper, tinned on the inside; large numbers of these were typically part of the equipment of wealthier houses. Tinplate versions provided a cheaper alternative and pewter moulds were also

ABOVE: *Moulds. (From left to right) Three earthenware jelly moulds; a pewter ice-cream mould; a tinplate pudding mould.*

RIGHT: *A pine jelly stand, height 855 mm (33½ inches). It belonged to a Miss Fuller who lived in Clifton, Bristol, and was used between 1900 and 1920.*

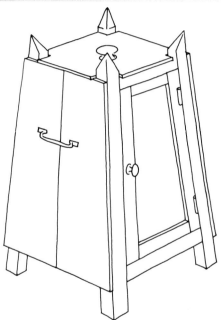

available, although, according to Mrs Beeton, earthenware moulds were preferable to those of tin or pewter for red jellies as the latter would spoil 'their colour and transparency'. From the 1880s jelly moulds of pressed glass, usually relatively simple in design, were introduced. At about the same time cheap substitutes for calves' foot jelly appeared, but were considered by some to possess an 'unpleasant flavour somewhat resembling glue'. The adoption of instant products together with the shortage of servants after the First World War caused a decline in domestic jellymaking and in turn to the status of jelly itself.

FURTHER READING

Beeton, Isabella. *Mrs Beeton's Book of Household Management.* 1861, and Chancellor Press, 1982.

Brears, P. *The Kitchen Catalogue.* York Castle Museum, 1979.

Brears, P. *Traditional Food in Yorkshire.* John Donald, 1987.

Campbell Franklin, L. *From Hearth to Cookstove.* House of Collectibles, 1978.

Church, R. A. *Kenricks in Hardware.* David & Charles, 1969.

Davies, Jennifer. *The Victorian Kitchen.* BBC Books, 1989.

Eveleigh, D. J. *Firegrates and Kitchen Ranges.* Shire, 1983, reprinted 1992.

Eveleigh, D. J. 'Put Down to a Clear Bright Fire – The English Tradition of Open Fire Roasting', *Folk Life*, 1991.

Eveleigh, D. J. 'Cooking Pots and Old Curios – Skillets and Posnets', *Folk Life*, 1994.

Kevill-Davies, S. *Jelly Moulds.* Lutterworth Press, 1983.

Seymour, J. *The National Trust Book of Forgotten Household Crafts*. Dorling Kindersley, 1987.
Seymour Lindsay, J. *Iron and Brass Implements of the English House*. Medici, 1927.
Wilson, C. A. *Food and Drink in Britain*. Peregrine, 1976.
Wilson, C. A. *Traditional Food East and West of the Pennines*. Edinburgh University Press, 1991.

PLACES TO VISIT

Many museums display old cooking utensils. Some of particular interest are listed here. Intending visitors are advised to find out opening times before making a special journey.

Anne of Cleves House Museum, 52 Southover High Street, Lewes, East Sussex. Telephone: 0273 474610.
Beamish, The North of England Open Air Museum, Beamish, County Durham DH9 0RG. Telephone: 0207 231811.
Blaise Castle House Museum, Henbury, Bristol BS10 7QS. Telephone: 0272 506789.
Cambridge and County Folk Museum, 2/3 Castle Street, Cambridge CB3 0AQ. Telephone: 0223 335159.
Cogges Manor Farm Museum, Church Lane, Cogges, Witney, Oxfordshire. Telephone: 0993 772602.
Erddig, Wrexham, Clwyd LL3 0YT. Telephone: 0978 355314.
Folk Museum, 99-103 Westgate Street, Gloucester GL1 2PG. Telephone: 0452 526467.
Ford Green Hall, Ford Green Road, Smallthorne, Stoke-on-Trent ST6 1NG. Telephone: 0782 534771.
Geffrye Museum, Kingsland Road, London E2 8EA. Telephone: 071-739 9893.
The Georgian House, 7 Great George Street, Bristol BS1 5RR. Telephone: 0272 211362.
Gustav Holst Birthplace Museum, 4 Clarence Road, Pittville, Cheltenham GL5 2AY. Telephone: 0242 524846.
Milton Keynes Museum of Industry and Rural Life, Southern Way, Wolverton, Milton Keynes MK12 5EJ. Telephone: 0908 316222 or 319148.
Museum of English Rural Life, University of Reading, Whiteknights, Reading RG6 2AG. Telephone: 0734 318660.
Number 1 Royal Crescent, Bath, Avon BA1 2LR. Telephone: 0225 428126.
Oxfordshire County Museum, Fletcher's House, Woodstock, Oxfordshire OX7 1SP. Telephone: 0993 811456.
Pallant House, 9 North Pallant, Chichester, Sussex PO19 1TJ. Telephone: 0243 774557.
Portsmouth City Museum and Art Gallery, Museum Road, Old Portsmouth PO1 2LJ. Telephone: 0705 827261.
Priest's House Museum, 23-27 High Street, Wimborne Minster, Dorset BH21 1HR. Telephone: 0202 882533.
The Royal Pavilion, Brighton, East Sussex BN1 1UE. Telephone: 0273 603005.
Rutland County Museum, Catmos Street, Oakham, Leicestershire. Telephone: 0572 723654.
Somerset Rural Life Museum, Abbey Farm, Chilkwell Street, Glastonbury, Somerset BA6 8DB. Telephone: 0458 831197.
Tudor House Museum, Friar Street, Worcester WR1 2NA. Telephone: 0905 20904.
Ulster Folk and Transport Museum, Cultra Manor, Holywood, Northern Ireland BT18 0EU. Telephone: 0232 428428.
Uppark, South Harting, near Petersfield, Hampshire. Telephone: 0730 825317/825458.
Wayside Museum, Old Mill House, Zennor, St Ives, Cornwall TR26 3DA. Telephone: 0736 796945.
Welsh Folk Museum, St Fagans, Cardiff CF5 6XB. Telephone: 0222 569441.
West Highland Museum, Cameron Square, Fort William PH33 6AJ. Telephone: 0397 702169.
York Castle Museum, Tower Street, York YO1 1RY. Telephone: 0904 653611.